COMPARISON
Trap

NORTH POINT
RESOURCES

© 2015 by North Point Ministries, Inc.
Cover script and interior layout designed by Anna Sanders.
Italics in Scripture quotations are the author's emphasis. Unless otherwise indicated, Scripture quotations are from: The Holy Bible, New International Version (NIV)
©1973, 1978, 1984, 2011 by Biblica, Inc.TM
Used by permission. All rights reserved worldwide. Printed in Canada.

Table of Contents

How to use

COMPARISON TRAP
IN A GROUP

---

1. WATCH:
As a group, watch the session video (20 minutes),
viewable from the DVD or App.

2. DISCUSS:
Talk through the corresponding Discussion Questions,
available in the *Comparison Trap Devotional*.

3. READ-WRITE-DRAW:
As group homework or on your own time,
read and complete the daily devotions and challenges.

foreword

by Charles F. Stanley

When my son, Andy, was born, his mother and I began praying that God would bring the right woman into Andy's life. Sandra is God's answer to our prayers. I've told Andy on more occasions than I can remember how blessed he is to have Sandra as his wife. She has not only been a fantastic wife to my son and mother to three of my grandchildren, she is an extraordinary person.

Being the wife of a pastor, especially a well-known pastor, is not an easy role to play. From day one, Sandra has stepped into that role with dignity and grace. For 27 years, I've watched her successfully navigate the complexity of being a pastor's wife. Andy would be quick to agree that he is a better pastor, father, and follower of Christ because of Sandra.

Until now, Sandra has chosen to stay out of the ministry spotlight. Other than volunteering at church on Sundays and serving with a local charity, her time and energy have been focused at home. Recently, however, Andy and Sandra became empty nesters. As Sandra prayed about what God would have her do in this next season, an opportunity surfaced for them to work together on this fantastic Bible study, *Comparison Trap*.

Like most fathers, I couldn't be prouder of my two children, Andy and Becky. And, of course, my six grandchildren have no equals. But as you are about to discover, I have every reason in the world to be a proud father-in-law as well. So, find yourself a pen or highlighter and a comfortable place to sit because you are about to be challenged, inspired, and encouraged by God's answer to my prayers those many years ago—*Sandra Stanley*.

Charles Stanley
Senior Pastor, First Baptist Church Atlanta
President, Founder, and CEO, In Touch Ministries

by Sandra Stanley

I didn't mean to have hair that looked like I had stuck my finger in a light socket. However, at around fifteen years old, I looked around and realized that my hair was stick straight in a world where curly hair was cool. What's a girl to do? Well, of course, ask her cousin who had just started attending beauty school to administer a perm. Why not? I could think of no good reason. So, off to the Dublin School of Beauticians I went.

In defense of my sweet cousin Vicki, it was a perfect storm of hitting puberty, getting a perm, and riding in a boat on Lake Sinclair for the afternoon. Oh . . . my . . . gosh! The radius of hair encircling my head was somewhere around ten inches. And, the perm lasted about seven years. I'm not kidding. My mom has pictures to prove it.

Comparison. It causes us to do some crazy stuff. Occasionally that crazy stuff is funny, but most of the time it's not.

A few years ago, Andy preached a sermon series entitled *Comparison Trap*. Powerful and life-altering are two adjectives I would use to describe its impact. We decided this series would be perfect for small groups, so a team of ladies went to work repurposing it into a four-week study designed specifically for women.

Andy might argue the point, but I think the temptation to compare is particularly relentless for women. We are quick to compare our appearances, our homes, our careers, our successes. We compare our boyfriends or husbands, our children. Good grief! What don't we compare? Often, we compare our pasts, our failures, and even our sins. It's exhausting and it's a thief of our peace.

But it doesn't have to be this way. We can get off the merry-go-round of comparison.

Since the temptation to compare bombards us incessantly, what better way to equip ourselves for battle than to daily renew our minds with insights and truths directly from Scripture. Thus, the book you're holding!

Each daily devotion will have a practical step to take or a question to think about throughout your day. It will point you back to Scripture—the most effective tool I've found against the trap of constant comparison. If you take advantage of these daily prompts, I think you'll find that twenty-one days from now, you will have developed a habit that will serve you well long after our study wraps up.

So, thank you for joining us for *Comparison Trap*. Let's do this together and discover how to break out of the trap. Instead of comparing, striving, and secretly celebrating the failures of others, you can take a deep breath and experience the peace that comes from understanding your extraordinary value to God, and that his plans for you are more than enough.

Sandra

Session One

Session One
DISCUSSION QUESTIONS

1. Get to know one another by sharing the following:
   - ☐ Your name
   - ☐ One fact about you
   - ☐ How you're hoping to benefit from the *Comparison Trap* study

2. Here are some examples of the "Land of -Er" that Andy listed:
   - ☐ Rich-er
   - ☐ Pretty-er
   - ☐ Skinny-er
   - ☐ Married-er
   - ☐ Smart-er

   Which are more prominent in the women you know? Do any of them ring true for you?

3. Sandra mentioned an example of comparison from elementary school. What is a memory you have of comparing yourself to others or being hurt by someone else's opinion of you?

4. Do you think that all comparison is bad?

5. In the video Sandra says, "Awareness drives our discontentment, and awareness isn't going away." Due to smartphones and social media, people are often too aware of the happenings in their friends' lives. What is something you can do to manage the jealousy that awareness can create?

6. In what ways have you seen comparison erode relationships?

DEVOTIONAL ⟹

week One
DAY ONE

*Love is patient, love is kind. It does not envy, it does
not boast, it is not proud.*
- 1 Corinthians 13:4

LOVE DOES not envy. It does not boast. It is not proud. These three things have something in common: each results from comparing ourselves to others. When I compare myself to someone who seems to have more, I lean into envy. When I compare myself to someone who has less, I open myself to the temptation of boastfulness and pride.

Have you ever chatted with a "one-upper"—someone who always has a bigger, better, more dramatic story to top yours? Or have you ever caught yourself thinking or saying, "Oh yeah, well wait until you hear this!"?

Today's verse reminds us that whether we're one of the "one-uppers" or we've just been "one-upped," love does not envy, it does not boast, it is not proud.

There is no win in comparison.

And there's no love in comparison either.

PRAYER:
Heavenly Father, thank you for loving me and for making clear what it means to love others. Let me be aware today of my tendency to allow comparison to send me to the unloving places of envy, boasting, and pride.

CHALLENGE

Challenge

IT'S EASY for our thoughts to drift in the direction of envy and pride. It's so much more difficult to intentionally speak words of kindness and patience. Work through the thoughts that come to your mind regarding envy and pride, and then think about some ways you can show patience and kindness today.

1. Fill in the blanks.

Envy and jealousy say . . .
I wish I had a

....

like hers.
Example: I wish I had a family like hers.

Pride and boasting say . . .
At least I have more

....

than she does.
Example: At least I have more money than she does.

Using these sentences, write your own answers in the boxes provided.

Instead of being envious and prideful . . .
I can be kind

to .... by ....

> *Example: I can be kind to **my husband** by **asking him about his day before I tell him about mine.***

I can be patient

with .... when ....

> *Example: I can be patient with **my daughter** when **she tries on five outfits before leaving for school.***

DAY TWO

*Whatever is true, whatever is noble, whatever is right,
whatever is pure, whatever is lovely, whatever is
admirable—if anything is excellent or praiseworthy—
think about such things.*
- Philippians 4:8

I'D LIKE to anchor this verse deeply in my heart. The apostle Paul, who wrote these words, understood that what we allow to linger in our minds will influence our words and actions. This is true for the good stuff and for the bad stuff.

When I spend time on social media viewing the photo-filtered highlights of my friends' lives, my thoughts don't usually end up being noble, pure, or lovely.

Discontentment can sometimes linger and even leak out.

Have you ever justified a shopping splurge—or even a home renovation—after envying what a friend has?

Even though Paul wrote this advice thousands of years ago, his encouragement to guard our thoughts is still good advice today. As he reminds us, we can choose what to think about. And we can choose to avoid what tempts us to compare.

What triggers your discontentment? Is it an app, a magazine, or a website? Is it a friend who always has the latest gossip? Is it a place? Maybe the playground where none of the other moms seem as frazzled as you?

Before you encounter that temptation, you can proactively choose to guard your thoughts. Rather than getting stuck in comparison's trap, today's verse reminds us to dwell instead on things that are true, noble, right, pure, lovely, admirable, excellent, and praiseworthy.

PRAYER:
God, thank you that words written so long ago still offer such wisdom today. Help me guard my mind and refocus my thoughts so that all my actions today honor you.

CHALLENGE

Challenge

ONE DAY away. One day away from the blogs you read and the apps you use. Think you can do it? Try—just for today—replacing your time online or on social media with time spent memorizing today's verse. Start now by writing it or drawing it on these pages. You could even write it on a card you can look at when you're tempted instead to look at your phone or computer.

1. Write out the verse word for word or in your own words.

Finally, brothers, whatever is true, whatever is noble, whatever is right, whatever is pure, whatever is lovely, whatever is admirable—if anything is excellent or praiseworthy—think about such things.
- Philippians 4:8

....

....

....

....

....

If you're the creative type, draw out this verse.
P.S. If you like what you draw, make it the home screen on your phone.

DAY THREE

I know what it is to be in need, and I know what it is to have plenty. I have learned the secret of being content in any and every situation, whether well fed or hungry, whether living in plenty or in want. I can do everything through him who gives me strength.
- Philippians 4:12–13

IF WE had to break out of the comparison trap by ourselves, we'd be doomed. The temptation to compare seems to be lurking around every corner. And just when we think we have it under control in one area, it seems to pop up in another!

So Paul's declaration that he's "learned the secret of being content in any and every situation" sounds a little like a too-good-to-be-true infomercial promise. But Paul's secret is, in fact, so effective that I'll offer you a "7-day money-back guarantee" if you'll try it.

The secret of contentedness is tapping into Christ's strength. So how do we do that? The most effective way I've found is to spend a few minutes of quiet time with God each morning.

The habit of praying and reading Scripture before my day gets going loads me up with the strength and perspective I need to resist the comparison trap.

When I've spent a few minutes in the morning thanking God for my kids, it's easier to resist envying my friend whose son just made the varsity team. And when I've spent time reading what God says about my worth and value, I don't feel insecure even if my friend's cooking skills outshine mine.

PRAYER:
Jesus, thank you that the secret of contentedness isn't something I have to earn or practice, but that I only need to ask for your help. Share your strength to keep me focused on you whether I'm "well fed or hungry, living in plenty or in want."

CHALLENGE

Challenge

GIVE YOUR first few minutes to God. Set your alarm for tomorrow morning just ten minutes earlier. (You can do this!) During those ten minutes, read back over Philippians 4:12–13 and ask God to help you conquer the comparison traps you'll face during your day. Writing helps me focus when my mind is tempted to wander (or go back to sleep!), so use this space to journal or write your prayer.

1. Once you've decided on the time you want to set your alarm tomorrow morning (we've got this, girls!), draw in the clock hands for the time you've landed on.

Okay, your alarm went off! Stretch, rub your eyes, and read this verse one more time. As random as your thoughts or prayer might be, write what comes to mind and a prayer asking God to help you conquer the comparison traps you'll face today.

I know what it is to be in need, and I know what it is to have plenty. I have learned the secret of being content in any and every situation, whether well fed or hungry, whether living in plenty or in want. I can do everything through him who gives me strength.
- Philippians 4:12-13

Week One

DAY FOUR

Better one handful with tranquility than two handfuls
with toil and chasing after the wind.
- Ecclesiastes 4:6

WHEN my kids were younger, they loved playing the game "Would You Rather?" My boys' questions seemed to always be choices between two terrible things, neither of which I would want to choose. With my daughter, the choices were sweeter, but that also made it difficult to pick! So, let's play this little game, shall we?

Would you rather get the promotion that everyone in the office is vying for or have consistent nights of dinner around the table with your family? Would you rather have a new, name-brand, trendy outfit or fall asleep easily without worrying about how to pay the next credit card bill? Would you rather have your thoughts consumed with how to move into the "perfect" neighborhood or have the mental energy to read to your kids before bedtime?

If your family were given the opportunity to answer those questions for you, I wonder what they would choose. Simply put, some things are more important than others. The wise woman recognizes that...

Choosing less of what doesn't last anyway leads to more of what matters most.

PRAYER:
Father, your ways are always better than mine. Lead me to make choices that honor you and ultimately bring tranquility and peace rather than toil and striving.

CHALLENGE

Challenge

WRITE DOWN some areas of your life in which you've been choosing "two handfuls with toil." Identify an action you can take today—declining an invitation, resigning from a committee, or pausing your plans—to instead choose "one handful with tranquility."

1. Complete the sentence below. Or, for you creative ladies, doodle your answers in the space provided.

I'm holding tightly to . . .
Examples: my reputation, my dreams

2. Answer the following questions.

 What could you give up today that would
bring you more peace?
Examples: resign from a committee, decline an invitation

 What would you gain by giving that up?
Examples: time at home with family, a much-needed nap

week One
DAY FIVE

And I saw that all labor and all achievement
spring from man's envy of his neighbor. This too is
meaningless, a chasing after the wind.
- Ecclesiastes 4:4

WHAT an amazing word picture: chasing after the wind. Can you picture yourself outside on a breezy day trying to catch the wind? You can tell which way it's going, but you can't ever hope to actually catch it. That's silly. What a waste of time.

That's the way it is with envy too. Envy accomplishes nothing.

We can spend lots of time on envy and end up with nothing to show for our efforts.

Have you ever tried a trendy new exercise routine? Maybe you bought the entire set of workout DVDs or a celebrity-endorsed contraption guaranteed to get results. If after a month of sweat and effort you hadn't dropped a dress size, your arms weren't any more toned, and your cholesterol levels hadn't budged, would you have continued with that routine? Of course not!

You can choose to end the worthless routine of comparison as well. It's meaningless, a waste of time. Let's decide today to recapture that wasted effort. Let's stop "chasing after the wind" and instead use our precious time more wisely.

PRAYER:
Father, please give me clarity today to recognize when I'm wasting time on comparison. Show me the worthwhile things I should focus my attention and effort on instead.

CHALLENGE

Challenge

USE THIS journal page to track when your mind tends to drift toward comparison and envy.

1. Fill in the lines below.

Three areas I frequently find myself stuck in the comparison trap:
Example: watching HGTV wishing I could renovate my house
        (Or maybe I'm the only one who does this.)

2. Rank the three areas you listed by how much time you spend. Hopefully, this will help you see your most significant comparison trap.

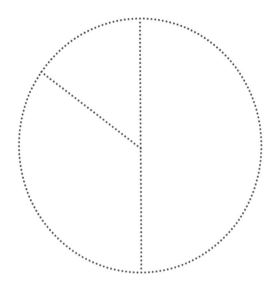

What's one thing I can do today to waste less time comparing?

Week One
DAY SIX

*Do not be anxious about anything, but in every
situation, by prayer and petition, with thanksgiving,
present your requests to God.*
- Philippians 4:6

DO YOU remember as a kid walking through a
parking lot with a friend or sibling when he or she
would yell, "Race you to the car!"? You didn't even
think about it; you just TOOK OFF! By the time you
reached the car, you were completely out of breath.
Comparison can be that way too.

Maybe you were strolling along at a comfortable pace
until you noticed something someone else bought. Or
maybe you heard about the latest accomplishment of a
friend's child. You were excited about your upcoming
beach trip until you heard about your neighbor's
Caribbean plans.

*And just like that,
you find yourself sprinting,
trying to catch up.*

You have to buy that thing. You feel an urgency to push your son into more activities for his résumé. Or you surf around online to upgrade your vacation.

It doesn't have to be this way. Instead of jumping into the race, how about dropping to your knees? I've found that many times the process of praying instead of racing takes away the desire for what I thought I wanted in the first place.

> "I go back to a phrase someone shared with me long ago, 'Not my race, not my pace.'"
> —Holley Gerth
> Blogger and Author, *You're Already Amazing*

PRAYER:
Heavenly Father, you didn't design me to be anxious or worried. Thank you for the way you have uniquely equipped me for my own race, not the race or the pace others are running.

CHALLENGE

Challenge

WRITE DOWN a few scenarios that challenge your sense of value and create anxiety. Then reevaluate those doubts and anxieties through the lens of gratitude, acknowledging what God has already done.

Fill in the lines below.

I feel anxious when ...
Example: my boss evaluates my performance against my peers

I am thankful for . . .
Example: a good job and a manager who challenges me

Week One

DAY SEVEN

*But if you harbor bitter envy and selfish ambition in
your hearts, do not boast about it or deny the truth.*

- James 3:14

SOMETIMES we like to dress up our bitter envy
and selfish ambition in nicer clothes. Instead of
owning the fact that they are ugly and admitting that
we need to rid ourselves of them, we spin it a little
differently.

*Are you pushing your
child or husband toward success
so that you can look
good to those around you?*

And rather than admitting it, you're dressing up
that selfish ambition as "helping them reach their

potential." Maybe you've gossiped about a friend's new health habits under the guise of "concern." But honestly, you're not concerned; you're jealous.

This game of justification robs us and our relationships of joy and peace. So today, let's just call it what it is and ask God to forgive us. Maybe there are some other people we love that we need to ask for forgiveness too.

PRAYER:
Heavenly Father, I confess my tendency to manipulate and push the people I care about most. My motivation has been selfish. Help me to stop dressing up my envy and ambition as something they are not.

CHALLENGE

Challenge

WHO HAVE you been hurting with your envy and ambition? Use these pages to begin drafting him or her a note of apology, confessing that your motivation has been selfish.

 Fill in the lines below.

> ···Who are you pushing toward success so you ··················
> can look good?

> ···What's one thing you can do today to celebrate ·············
> that person?

You guessed it: a word search.

BITTERNESS	AMBITION	GOSSIP
ENVY	SUCCESS	JEALOUS
SELFISH	BOAST	MANIPULATE

```
G  Y  W  Y  L  T  S  H  O  Q
E  I  A  W  A  U  B  S  T  C
O  P  Z  M  C  P  U  I  G  Z
D  W  N  C  W  R  S  F  O  G
V  E  E  O  N  W  X  L  C  J
N  S  M  Q  I  Q  N  E  Y  Q
S  P  Y  Z  F  T  D  S  L  P
P  P  S  G  V  J  I  S  X  L
E  J  U  S  V  W  M  B  N  W
T  Q  O  S  C  K  J  E  M  R
A  F  L  E  H  G  V  E  T  A
L  T  A  N  D  T  H  D  X  V
U  Y  E  R  W  S  J  U  U  F
P  V  J  E  P  W  J  F  B  J
I  N  K  T  S  A  O  B  B  Q
N  E  O  T  T  Y  K  N  O  I
A  C  P  I  S  S  O  G  O  W
M  B  K  B  M  O  Q  Y  G  O
H  M  Y  K  P  A  O  X  M  G
E  S  E  U  A  T  I  Z  T  U
```

There is no win in comparison.

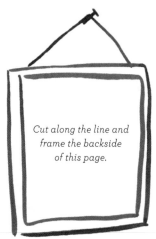

Cut along the line and frame the backside of this page.

Session
two

Session two
DISCUSSION QUESTIONS

1. What were your parents like growing up? How do you think that may have affected you?

2. Is it difficult or comforting for you to refer to God as "Father"?

3. Why do you think we value the opinion of our friends or loved ones more than God's?

4. How does comparison trick you into completing this statement: If I had _____, I would be more valuable. (Example: If I had a better body, I would be more valuable.)

5. Read these verses aloud in your group.

   "[God] created my inmost being . . . I am fearfully and wonderfully made." - Psalm 139:14

   "Before I formed you in the womb I knew you, before you were born I set you apart." - God, Jeremiah 1:5

   "[I] will take great delight in you . . . and rejoice over you with singing." - God, Zephaniah 3:17

   How might these truths contradict the way you naturally view yourself?

DEVOTIONAL

DAY ONE

But God demonstrates his own love for us in this: While we were still sinners, Christ died for us.
- Romans 5:8

In him we have redemption through his blood, the forgiveness of sins, in accordance with the riches of God's grace that he lavished on us with all wisdom and understanding.
- Ephesians 1:7-8

Very truly I tell you, the one who believes has eternal life.
- John 6:47

THESE verses are EVERYTHING. Read them slowly and let their truths settle into your heart.

Those of us who are flea market and thrift shop bargainers know that the value of a thing is determined by the price it will bring. And God redeemed you—paid for you—with his own Son. Your value to your heavenly Father is incomprehensible.

If you've never done it before, find a quiet place and a quiet moment, bow before him, and accept his most precious gift—your salvation.

Because God was willing to sacrifice his Son for you, he has declared once and for all that you are worthy.

You are valuable. You are precious to him. He says to you, "You are fine because you are mine."

PRAYER:
Heavenly Father, thank you for the extraordinary value you've placed on me as evidenced by the price you were willing to pay. When I let that settle in my heart, it melts me. I am filled with gratitude for the salvation you offered me through the death and resurrection of your Son, Jesus. I humbly accept your gift. Thank you that in your eyes I am forgiven and fine because I belong to you.

CHALLENGE

Challenge

DO YOU have a friend who could use a reminder of her value to God? Use these pages to write out some of the ways she is valuable to you and to God. Once you have your thoughts on paper, write her a card or take a picture of these pages and text the photo to her.

1. Fill in the lines below.

I want to encourage ....

She is amazing because . . .

☙ ....

☙ ....

☙ ....

☙ ....

☙ ....

2. Write a quick note to your friend in this space. Then take a picture and send it to her. You'll make her day!

DAY TWO

*Do not conform any longer to the pattern of this world,
but be transformed by the renewing of your mind. Then
you will be able to test and approve what God's will
is—his good, pleasing and perfect will.*

- Romans 12:2

THE STRUGGLE with comparison is really a struggle with lies, isn't it? It's a lie that we don't measure up to those around us. It's a lie that what others have diminishes what we have. It's a lie that the pretty photos we see of our friends' lives accurately depict their everyday realities.

When we simply drift in the direction culture takes us, we end up stuck in the trap of lies.

We find ourselves conformed "to the pattern of this world." But today's verse gives us an action step to escape that trap—renewing our minds.

So how do we do that? Renewing your mind is an ongoing process of identifying a lie and then replacing it with truth from God. And, you're already getting a great start! Filling our minds with the truths of Scripture, like we've been doing each day together, is THE most effective way to battle the lies of comparison.

PRAYER:
Father, thank you for the truth that you've created me uniquely and you don't expect me to be anyone else. Give me the patience and persistence needed to replace lies with the timeless truths of your words.

CHALLENGE

Challenge

Complete the exercise below. Then work this week to memorize the scriptural truth for the lie you struggle with most.

 1. Check any of the statements below that you sometimes believe about yourself. If you check more than one, you're in good company!

☐ It's important that other people think I am smart/pretty/talented/successful/a good mom, etc.

☐ If only I had _____, I would be happy.

☐ I can't let other people see my failures or flaws.

☐ I can control my reputation.

☐ I should feel guilty about having so much when others have so little.

☐ I like being the best at whatever I do.

☐ As I compare my skills and abilities to the women around me, I don't measure up.

☐ I must be doing something wrong since God isn't giving me what I want.

Find the statements that you marked to sometimes be true of you. Then spend some time reading the truths that are opposite of those lies. Hopefully, these truths will encourage you.

It's important that other people think I am smart/pretty/talented/successful/a good mom, etc.	*The Lord does not look at the things people look at. People look at the outward appearance, but the Lord looks at the heart.* 1 Samuel 16:7
If only I had _____, I would be happy.	*And my God will meet all your needs according to the riches of his glory in Christ Jesus.* Philippians 4:19
I can't let other people see my failures or flaws.	*But [God] said to me, "My grace is sufficient for you, for my power is made perfect in weakness."* 2 Corinthians 12:9
I can control my reputation.	*Am I now trying to win the approval of human beings, or of God? Or am I trying to please people? If I were still trying to please people, I would not be a servant of Christ.* Galatians 1:10
I should feel guilty about having so much when others have so little.	*Every good and perfect gift is from above, coming down from the Father.* James 1:17
I like being the best at whatever I do.	*In humility consider others better than yourselves, not looking to your own interests but each of you to the interests of others.* Philippians 2:3–4
As I compare my skills and abilities to the women around me, I don't measure up.	*We have different gifts, according to the grace given to each of us.* Romans 12:6
I must be doing something wrong since God isn't giving me what I want.	*In their hearts humans plan their course, but the Lord establishes their steps.* Proverbs 16:9

DAY THREE

Blessed are the pure in heart, for they will see God.
- Matthew 5:8

I LOVE the truth in this simple beatitude that Jesus taught his followers. Blessed—or in other words, happy or at rest—are those people who have pure hearts. A pure heart allows us to recognize God's gifts, to discern his will, to feel his nudging. But a pure heart takes a little work. And comparison is constantly trying to muddy it up again.

Greed to own what friends own can drive us into debt. Jealousy over our husbands' long hours at work can erode our relationships. Envy of friends getting engaged can wreck our self-esteem. These are all heart problems that will grow out of a habit of comparison left unchecked.

So what do you do to keep a pure heart? You can start by avoiding the entertainment and images that tempt you to compare. You can confess when envy leads you to boasting and pride. And you can work hard on the habit of cleaning out your heart when temptations, like comparison, muddy it up.

Above all else, guard your heart, for everything you do flows from it.

Proverbs 4:23

PRAYER:
Heavenly Father, I so very much want a pure heart. I commit today to doing the work it takes to clean out the comparison and other temptations that make it harder to see you and your will for me.

CHALLENGE

Challenge

Use the following questions to give your heart a check-up today. Bonus: If you're a parent, teach your children the value of keeping clean hearts by making these questions a regular part of your bedtime routine.

◎ Today is a heart check-up. Try and answer these questions honestly.

Who am I jealous of?

In what area do I feel like I'm falling behind?

Whose failure do I secretly celebrate?

In what area am I currently dissatisfied?

What lie about myself do I keep believing?

What is tempting me to make an unwise decision?

DAY FOUR

But the Lord said to Samuel, "Do not consider his appearance or his height, for I have rejected him. The Lord does not look at the things people look at. People look at the outward appearance, but the Lord looks at the heart."
- 1 Samuel 16:7

WHEN another driver's behavior behind the wheel annoys me, rather than get angry, I try to guess the story of his or her day. For example, that speeder who just swerved past me is probably rushing to the hospital to meet his wife who's in labor. Do you do this too? Making up a justification—even if it's just made up—somehow takes the bite out of my reaction.

This game of grace-giving can also take the sting out of comparison. Maybe her engagement ring is so big because the stone is a family heirloom. Maybe her fancy SUV is the only car that makes her feel safe after a scary car accident.

The truth is . . .

We can't see what's going on in other people's hearts. But God can.

In today's passage, the prophet Samuel had in mind the kind of person, the kind of look, the kind of talents a future king should have. God, however, had other ideas. God assured Samuel that he doesn't see people the way the world does. He knows the whole story.

So the next time you're tempted to let the insecurities of comparison derail you, remember that God sees differently; he knows her whole story and your whole story. He is quietly whispering to you, "You're fine because you're mine."

PRAYER:
God, I'm so grateful that you don't see us the way we sometimes see one another. Place the reminder in my heart today that only you know my whole story, so comparison is a useless pursuit.

CHALLENGE

Challenge

WRITE DOWN the last scenario in which comparison made you feel inadequate. Then imagine a graceful justification for why she has what you want. If your made-up story were true, would you still feel insecure about how you measure up to her?

1. Think about a time this last week when you felt you didn't measure up or you weren't enough. Here's an example.

> I felt I wasn't
>
> *creative*
>
> enough when ...
>
> *another mom brought Pinterest-worthy cupcakes in for the classroom birthday party.*
>
>

2. Now write your own example or memory in this space.

> I felt I wasn't
>
> ....
>
> enough when . . .

3. Renew your mind to the truth that God sees you as a woman of great worth. Rather than looking around for the approval of others, you can look to him for all your worth and affirmation.

DAY FIVE

*For we are God's masterpiece. He has created us
anew in Christ Jesus, so we can do the good things he
planned for us long ago.*
- Ephesians 2:10

ARE YOU aware that God considers you his masterpiece? Isn't that amazing? Not only that, but this jackpot of truth also says that God had a plan for you from the beginning of time.

Do you remember how you felt when you discovered that all your fifth-grade friends had a sleepover and you weren't invited? That may have been years ago, but comparison can draw us right back to that exact feeling. Watching a friend receive or achieve something you've desperately wished for leaves you asking the exact same question you asked in fifth grade: Why not me?

I find incredible comfort in what today's verse says: God has "good things . . . planned for us long ago." The good things—the plans, the blessings, the circumstances—that he's picked for me aren't the same as yours. There's an answer to comparison's question, "Why not me?" God has something else planned for you—something even more perfectly suited to your skills, gifts, and temperament.

You need only to . . .

Take your cue about you from the one who made you, loves you, redeemed you . . . and the one who calls you his masterpiece.

PRAYER:
Father, when I get stuck looking to my left or looking to my right, help me remember to take my cue only from you. I'm so humbled that you love me enough to have picked out plans specifically for me.

CHALLENGE

Challenge

WRITE DOWN the name of a friend who recently received or achieved something you've been wishing for. Reach out with a phone call, note, or text celebrating her. Then spend a few minutes praying for clarity about what God has planned for you.

1. Who received or achieved something you've been wishing you had? Write her name and what she has that you want. Be honest!

2. Write a quick celebration note to the woman you just listed. Here's an example...

> How much do you love your new car?
> I've always thought that car was beautiful.
> You look great driving it!

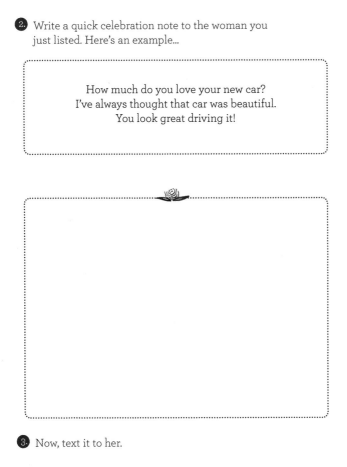

3. Now, text it to her.

DAY SIX

We demolish arguments and every pretension that sets itself up against the knowledge of God, and we take captive every thought to make it obedient to Christ.

- 2 Corinthians 10:5

I LIVE in suburban Atlanta now but grew up in middle Georgia. My grandparents lived on a farm. A few years ago, I decided to embrace my farm-girl heritage and take up gardening. I prepped a plot of dark, rich soil. I planted tomatoes, cucumbers, okra, squash, and beans. I watched the sky for signs of rain. Then I got busy with other things. When I returned to my garden a few days later, there were weeds everywhere.

The more weeds I pulled, the more seemed to return in their place. The harvest was incredible, worth all the effort. But I have to tell you, weeding was a constant part of the process.

Keeping our minds renewed isn't so different. Like staying on top of weeds, it's an active process. I love the wording Paul uses in this verse: "We take every thought captive."

When comparison, jealousy, and insecurity lodge thoughts in our minds, we can capture those thoughts.

We can identify them as lies and replace them with scriptural truth. Just like gardening, the harvest of a healthy mind and heart will be worth all the effort.

PRAYER:
Heavenly Father, remind me today of the importance of vigilantly taking unhealthy thoughts captive. Thank you for giving me an entire book of truth so I can replace my unhealthy thoughts with ones that honor you.

CHALLENGE

Challenge

REFER BACK to the exercise you completed on page 53 earlier this week. If you've successfully memorized one scriptural truth, choose another. Start by writing or drawing it in today's journal space.

Below is one of my favorite verses from page 53. Write or draw your favorite verse in the space on the next page.

In humility consider others better than yourselves, not looking to your own interests but each of you to the interests of others.

PHILIPPIANS 2:3-4

DAY SEVEN

*Now to him who is able to do immeasurably more than
all we ask or imagine, according to his power that is
at work within us, to him be glory in the church and in
Christ Jesus throughout all generations, forever and
ever! Amen.*
- Ephesians 3:20-21

THE FIRST part of this verse always gets my
attention. I love the idea of God doing immeasurably
more than I could ever ask. I love that he has the power
to do more for me than I could even dream up.

But guess what? This verse isn't really about him doing
stuff for me. Look at the second part. This is what the
verse is about: God being glorified forever.

Can I push you a little? Do comparison and envy and
boasting and insecurity bring glory to God? His power
can work through you to accomplish more than you
can even conceive of. Why spend your time stuck in
the mess caused by comparison?

We are called to a much higher, much more noble purpose than keeping up with those around us. Our days can be spent bringing glory to God.

There's no time to waste looking to our left or our right.

We can serve our neighbors, open our doors, and make room at our messy tables. Then when God accomplishes more than we can dream, we can watch him get the glory.

PRAYER:
Heavenly Father, I want my life to glorify you. Remind me today that my thoughts, words, and actions are best used to bring you glory and guard me from the tempting trap of comparison.

CHALLENGE

Challenge

WRITE a list below of occasions when God answered your prayers with more than you could have ever asked. Spend a few minutes thanking and praising him for exercising his power on your behalf. Then refer back to this list when the temptation to compare distracts you from more worthwhile pursuits.

1. Write how you would finish this sentence.

God came through (big time) for me when...

....

....

....

....

....

....

....

....

If you would rather draw your answer, use this space.

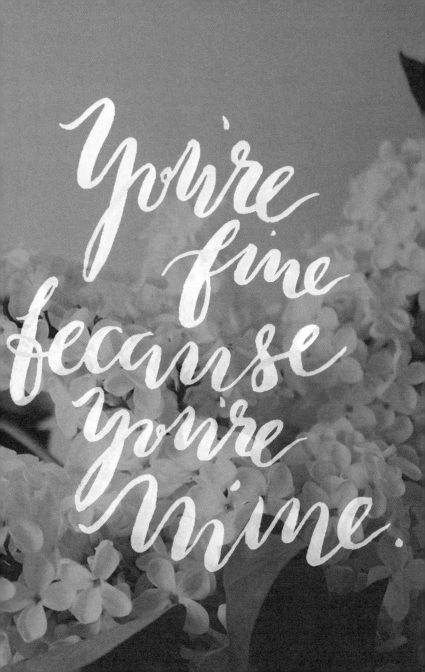

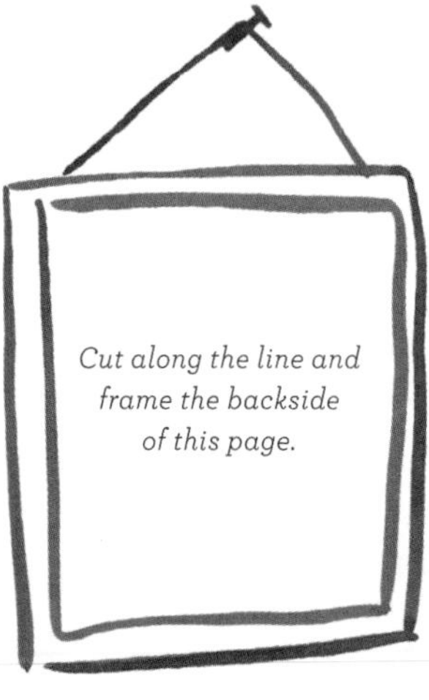

*Cut along the line and
frame the backside
of this page.*

Session
Three

Session three
DISCUSSION QUESTIONS

1. Do you more often compare yourself to people in a better or worse place than you?

2. In what area of your life do you feel blessed, like the servant who received five bags of gold?

3. What is something in your life story that is just plain hard to accept—a "one-bagger" situation?

4. Is it possible that the situation you mentioned in the previous question could be used to positively help someone else? If yes, in what way?

5. Andy recapped the parable by saying, "The Master determined who got what." How does it make you feel to know that God is going to give more to some people and less to others?

DEVOTIONAL

DAY ONE

But the fruit of the Spirit is love, joy, peace, patience, kindness, goodness, faithfulness, gentleness, and self-control. Against such things there is no law.
- Galatians 5:22-23

"EVERY MINUTE you spend comparing yourself to others is a minute you spend subtly accusing God of shortchanging you." This insight is so convicting for me!

My kids are past the stage of life that includes blowout birthday parties. But those of you in the parenting trenches may recognize this scene: your sweet kid has been the celebrated center of attention all day; the candles have been blown out; the heaping mound of presents has been unwrapped. And yet, there are tears. That mound of presents didn't include the one thing your child absolutely had to have.

Do you think our habit of comparison might make God feel like a parent listening to a post-party meltdown? Today's verse tells us that God has given us—through the Holy Spirit—the gifts of love, joy, peace, patience, kindness, goodness, faithfulness, gentleness, and self-control. Those gifts should leave us feeling anything but shortchanged!

So this week, when disappointment from comparison begins seeping into your heart, remember . . .

God has already given you peace, patience, and self-control—the very gifts you need to escape comparison's trap.

PRAYER:
God, I admit that it's so easy to focus on what I don't have and forget the incredible gifts you've given me. But I am so thankful that even though I don't deserve it, your generosity has richly equipped me.

CHALLENGE

Challenge

SOME OF the fruits of the spirit are more difficult to tap into than others, wouldn't you agree? Think through some recent scenarios where comparison got the best of you. How could you have responded better had you been tuned in to the Holy Spirit?

1. Read through these examples.

Example:
My mother-in-law criticized my cooking, which annoyed me.
> **LOVE says, "Dinner was a little dry tonight, sorry about that."**

My best friend booked her Caribbean vacation, and although it's out of our budget, I think we'll join them.
> **SELF-CONTROL says, "The Caribbean sounds nice, but we can't afford it this year."**

My younger sister just bought a new house; my husband and I are still renting.
> **PEACE says, "I'm content with the rented roof over my head and excited for my little sister."**

2. Your Turn. Write out your own example(s) of a time in your life when you really could have used one of the fruits of the Spirit.

DAY TWO

Let us not become conceited, or provoke one another,
or be jealous of one another.
- Galatians 5:26

WE'VE TALKED a lot about comparing ourselves
to others and being dissatisfied with the findings. But
what about when you get a glimpse of someone and
the scales tilt in the other direction? You decide you're
better than . . . prettier than . . . smarter than. That's no
less dangerous, is it?

Coming out on top in comparison's game can lead you
to conceit, arrogance, and pride. Or it can leave you
like my friend, who after working and saving for years,
then weathering traumatic family circumstances, was
filled with guilt when she finally moved into her dream
home with her healthy, happy family.

God's blessings are not supposed to come with strings of arrogance or guilt attached.

So how do we avoid these pitfalls? God has already given us the tools we need to snip those strings. Look back at yesterday's list of the fruits of the spirit.

Joy, kindness, goodness, gentleness . . . these sound to me like exact opposites of the conceit and jealousy we're warned against today. To steward God's blessings well, we just need to display outwardly the qualities of the Spirit that already live inside us.

PRAYER:
Heavenly Father, when the measuring stick shows that I have more, will you remind me that everything I have comes from you? Thank you that you not only give me great blessings, but you also give me your Spirit to help me steward those blessings well.

CHALLENGE

Challenge

WRITE DOWN one thing for which you've taken the credit that actually belongs to God. (Hint: what was the last thing you bragged about?) Then, write out what you think it would look like, instead, to handle that blessing with joy, kindness, goodness, and gentleness.

1. What's the last thing you bragged about?
   Hint: your kids, your house, your vacation

Consider this:

Every good and perfect gift is from above, coming down from the Father.
James 1:17

2. How might knowing that the thing you brag about is
a gift from God change your thoughts and actions?

THOUGHTS:

ACTIONS:

DAY THREE

Andrew spoke up, "Here is a boy with five small barley loaves and two small fish, but how far will they go among so many?" Jesus said, "Have the people sit down." There was plenty of grass in that place, and they sat down (about five thousand men were there). Jesus then took the loaves, gave thanks, and distributed to those who were seated as much as they wanted. He did the same with the fish. When they had all had enough to eat, he said to his disciples, "Gather the pieces that are left over. Let nothing be wasted." So they gathered them and filled twelve baskets with the pieces of the five barley loaves left over by those who had eaten.
- Galatians 5:26

WHEN YOU think about the fact that five small barley loaves and two small fish actually fed an estimated ten thousand people (including women and children), it's astounding! The story of this miracle never ceases to amaze me.

But what about the boy? I wonder what he thought about the miracle happening right in front of him. I picture him standing close to Jesus, wide-eyed and looking back and forth from his little container to the twelve baskets of leftovers.

What did it do to the boy's faith to watch Jesus turn his small offering into a blessing for so many others? What could it do to your faith to watch God do the same with what you can offer?

Let's promise to fight the feeling that our little bits could never go far enough. (Doesn't that discouragement come easily in our age of posted pictures and social media streams?) Let's instead trust God to make it astoundingly more.

Just like the boy at the center of the miracle . . .

What you have is less important than what you do with what you have.

PRAYER:
Father, help me learn that whether a lot or a little, the amount doesn't matter. May I always be willing to allow you to take what I have and make it immeasurably more.

CHALLENGE

Challenge

THINK FOR a minute about the boy and his two small fish. Did he know how Jesus would use them? Work through these questions and see how this story has application for you today.

1. What are your "two small fish"? Write them here. It could be a gift or talent, free time, extra money, etc.

2. Rather than focusing on HOW God might use what you have, what if you stepped out in faith and offered your two fish to God—even without knowing what might happen? How might that grow your faith?

3. Now, call a friend or discuss in next week's group how you could start sharing your two fish with others.

DAY FOUR

Then he said to them, "Watch out! Be on your guard
against all kinds of greed; a man's life does not consist
in the abundance of his possessions."
- Luke 12:15

WE LIVE in a world of accumulation. We have
closets, pantries, basements, garages, sheds, and even
storage units that we pay for each month. Good grief!
It's no wonder we struggle with thinking that our
lives actually do "consist in the abundance of [our]
possessions."

Jesus had more to say about this in the parable that
immediately follows today's verse.

And he told them this parable: "The ground of a certain
rich man yielded an abundant harvest. He thought to
himself, 'What shall I do? I have no place to store my
crops.' Then he said, 'This is what I'll do. I will tear down
my barns and build bigger ones, and there I will store my
surplus grain. And I'll say to myself, "You have plenty of
grain laid up for many years. Take life easy; eat, drink,
and be merry."' But God said to him, 'You fool! This very
night your life will be demanded from you. Then who will
get what you have prepared for yourself?' This is how it
will be with whoever stores up things for themselves but is
not rich toward God."
- Luke 12:16-21

You and I may not be able to relate to having a surplus of grain or needing bigger barns, but how many of us have surpluses of shoes or clothes for which we've dreamed of building extravagant closets?

In this parable, Jesus illustrates that . . .

the accumulation of more is a worthless pursuit if what you are accumulating isn't put to good use for God.

We all have a surplus of something. What can you do to leverage yours? What should you be sharing instead of storing up? What would it look like for you to be "rich toward God" by being generous to others?

PRAYER:
Father, I don't want to make the same mistake as the rich man in the parable, storing up what I should be sharing with others. Help me be on guard against this greed and recognize opportunities to be generous.

CHALLENGE

Challenge

OUR CULTURE of accumulation convinces us that we don't have enough. Let's take a quick inventory, shall we?

1. Check all the boxes that apply to you.

I currently have:

☐ A PANTRY STOCKED WITH FOOD   ☐ A COMFORTABLE BED
☐ A HOUSE FOR MY CAR (GARAGE)   ☐ A WASHING MACHINE
☐ MORE THAN ONE REFRIGERATOR   ☐ PAID TIME OFF
☐ A ROOF OVER MY HEAD   ☐ A GUEST ROOM
☐ CENTRAL AIR CONDITIONING   ☐ INDOOR PLUMBING
☐ TIME TO KILL ON SOCIAL MEDIA   ☐ FREE TIME
☐ ACCESS TO MEDICAL CARE   ☐ A CONSISTENT PAYCHECK
☐ A CAR   ☐ MEANINGFUL RELATIONSHIPS

Wow—look at all the things you have. Our awareness of what everyone else has drives us to want more. More clothes, bigger houses, expensive vacations. While we're busy wanting and accumulating more, we ignore what we already have and neglect to use our blessings for good.

2. Answer the following questions.

What are some areas that you can acknowledge having a surplus?

What would it look like to be "rich toward God" by being generous toward others?

Examples:
Provide a meal for a family in need.
A colleague at work doesn't have access to a car; drive her to work.
Open your home for a neighborhood event.

DAY FIVE

*All the days ordained for me were written in your book
before one of them came to be.*

- Psalm 139:16

A COUPLE of summers ago, I decided to memorize Psalm 139. It's a chapter rich with truth and encouragement, and today's verse is my very favorite in the whole chapter. I love the way it beautifully emphasizes the fact that . . .

*God isn't just aware of me.
He created me thoughtfully
and laid out a plan
for my life.*

It's fun to picture God picking out the opportunities that would perfectly fit each of us. When we get stuck in the comparison trap, though, envy and jealousy can trick us into thinking that when God ordained our days, he had a limited number of blessings to distribute—that when a friend achieves success, there's a little less for us.

With our God, nothing could be further from the truth. Yes, God's plan for your friend may include the husband you're still waiting for or the children you pray for month after month. But today's verse reminds you that if you're busy glancing to the left and right, jealous of someone else's plan, you'll miss the perfect one he's written just for you.

PRAYER:
Heavenly Father, it's so tempting to compare the plan you've laid out for me to your plans for my friends—especially when I feel like I'm falling behind. Let me be constantly reminded that glancing to my left and right will only distract me from the opportunities you've ordained for me.

CHALLENGE

Challenge

THINK of a time an unanswered prayer was disappointing in the short-term but in hindsight you saw it was for the best. Write what you remember and how you felt. Use this situation as a reminder of God's plan for you next time you catch yourself discouraged by someone else's success.

⊙ Take some time to think and journal through these questions.

What do I remember about my unanswered prayer?

How did I feel about my unanswered prayer?

How did that unanswered prayer change
my relationship with God?

DAY SIX

But godliness with contentment is great gain. For we brought nothing into the world and we can take nothing out of it. But if we have food and clothing, we will be content with that.
- 1 Timothy 6:6-8

IN A RECENT sermon, Andy mentioned the fact that no one, at the time of death, wants to take one last look at his fancy car. No one asks to have her jewelry brought in so that she can say her goodbyes. No one asks to be reminded of how many Twitter or Instagram followers he or she has accumulated. In those moments, the "stuff" of life loses significance.

"We brought nothing into the world and we can take nothing out of it." When we think this through, we find that the things we tend to compare are the things that fall away in the end, aren't they?

How do we remember that when we get caught up fretting over the small stuff? Today's verse tells us the answer is contentment.

the shortcut to contentment is gratitude.

If you start your day thanking God for the strong, capable body he's given you, later comparing your thighs to someone else's would feel a bit silly, wouldn't it? Try this shortcut and see if it doesn't adjust your perspective for the better.

PRAYER:
Jesus, I admit that I can get distracted by things that won't last; yet I am blessed with more than I could ever need to be content. Thank you for my incredible family, my loyal friends, my gifts, time, talent, and treasures.

CHALLENGE

Challenge

THINK back over the last 24 hours. Write down all the things you compared to someone else. Then put a line through the things that won't be significant in the long-term—the things that won't matter when you're on your deathbed. Are there any items left on your list?

1. List five things you compared to someone else.

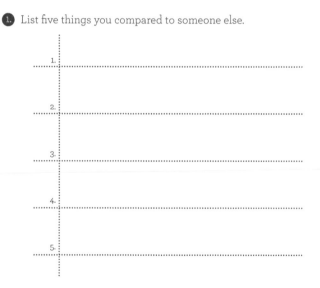

1.

2.

3.

4.

5.

2. List five things that will be important to you on your last day.

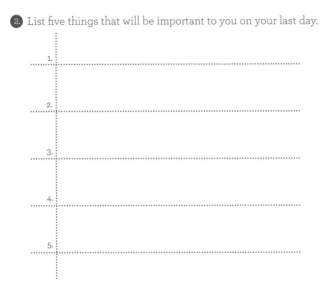

1.

2.

3.

4.

5.

Think about this for a minute: Which column had
more "things" and which had more "relationships"?

DAY SEVEN

But seek first his kingdom and his righteousness, and
all these things will be given to you as well.
- Matthew 6:33

IN MATTEW 6, Jesus devotes a whole section of his Sermon on the Mount to worry. I wonder why? We all worry a little (okay, a lot), don't we? We worry about our futures. We worry about our health. We worry about our families. We worry about our appearances and reputations. And when we look around and see what everyone else has and what everyone else is doing, we worry that we're falling behind.

Jesus knows us so well. He pokes a hole in our bad habit with a great question. "Who of you by worrying can add a single hour to his life?" In other words, it's a waste of time to worry. It isn't going to help one bit.

So if worrying doesn't help, what does? Jesus says, "Seek first his kingdom." Translation: God's plans trump mine.

Worry is a crutch for things we can't control.

But submitting to God's plan gives the control to God. And feeling confident about how God wants you to live makes it impossible to simultaneously feel insecure about how you measure up to others.

PRAYER:
Father, when worry starts creeping into my thoughts, please double my confidence in your plans for me. Thank you for being so worthy and so reliable that I have no need for pointless, time-wasting worry.

CHALLENGE

Challenge

WHAT are your two biggest categories of worry (e.g., family, finances, health)? Write down each worry and one action step you can take this week to seek God's will as it relates to each one. Maybe you need to spend time in prayer, read a book, or talk with a wise friend over coffee.

1. Think about how you would complete these phrases. Then write what came to your mind.

{I worry about...}   {I could take action by...}

WORRY	ACTION

 If you have another worry on your mind, use this space to keep writing your thoughts.

WORRY	ACTION

the shortcut to contentment is gratitude.

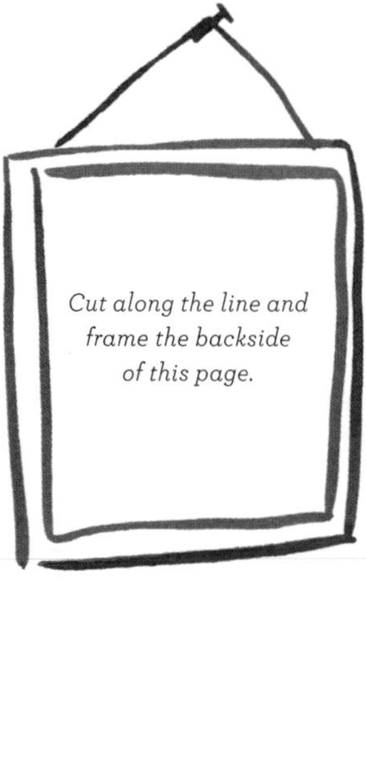

*Cut along the line and
frame the backside
of this page.*

Session Four

Session four
DISCUSSION QUESTIONS

1. In the message, Andy uses the items on a bookshelf to represent the different aspects of our lives that define who we are. Talk about the items on your bookshelf: career, health, money, talent, family, skills, etc. How have they shaped you?

2. What is the one item on your bookshelf that is unique to you—the thing that makes you different from everyone else?

3. Can you remember a time when you were celebrated *out loud* and *on purpose*?

4. How could your life look different if you could stop comparing?

5. What is one thing you can do this week to begin leveraging what God has entrusted to you?

DEVOTIONAL

DAY ONE

*Where you have envy and selfish ambition, there you
find disorder and every evil practice.*
- James 3:16

IMAGINE that a friend tells you her husband got a
promotion at work. By the time she's finished the story,
you've pictured the amazing vacations and new house they'll
probably buy. You've wondered if she'll quit her job to stay
home with the kids. And you've decided to chat with your
husband about updating his résumé. You've pulled out
comparison's measuring stick and decided that your family
has fallen short.

If James, the author of today's verse, could speak to you in
that moment, he'd say, "You're not thinking straight!"

Envy and selfishness create disorder—in our minds at first, and eventually in our actions.

My friend Kay Wyma wrote a book called *I'm Happy for You (Sort Of . . . Not Really)*. Ha! Doesn't that just capture it? In the book, she encourages her readers to move from a "wish it was me" mentality to an "I'm happy for you" out-loud declaration.

Kay knows the power of celebrating others out loud and on purpose—even when our words and thoughts don't exactly match. Choosing to celebrate your friends' good news (and it's a choice) is the quickest, most powerful antidote to envy.

PRAYER:
Heavenly Father, when I find myself comparing and then withholding words that would bless someone, would you please remind me to consider humbly moving in her direction?

CHALLENGE

Challenge

HOW EASY it is for us to drift toward things in our lives that steal our joy. These questions will help you think through how you're feeling and what you're thinking today.

Time for another heart check-up. Grab a cup of coffee and your favorite pen and work your way through these questions.

Whose success have I been hesitant to celebrate?

Why was I hesitant to celebrate her?

What insecurities surfaced in me
when I learned about her success?

Why am I insecure about those areas?

DAY TWO

*Do nothing out of selfish ambition or vain conceit,
but in humility consider others better than yourselves.
Each of you should look not only to your own interests,
but to the interests of others.*
- Philippians 2:2-4

ANDY AND I have two sons who love baseball; they both played for years, each as pitchers. As parents, it was nearly impossible not to compare our boys to the opposing team's pitcher during any given game. Frequently, the other pitcher was better. Here's what Andy shared in his book *Enemies of the Heart.*

I always make a point of tracking down the other pitcher and telling him what a great job he did. And when I can figure out whose son he is, I congratulate the parents too. It's a habit that keeps my heart free and clear. Reaching out my hand to shake the hand of another father whose son out-pitched mine releases all that negative energy and puts everything back into perspective.

There's something powerful and liberating about celebrating the success of other people.

When a person or topic is a particularly sensitive trigger for you (e.g., she loses ten pounds after you've yo-yo dieted for years), it's going to take more than polite words of celebration ("Good for you!") to clean out your heart.

We talked yesterday about celebrating others out loud and on purpose; let's go one step further today to take tangible action to celebrate our deserving friends.

PRAYER:
God, show me what I can do to put the "interests of others" above my own. Open my eyes to ways I can act with humility when comparison triggers my selfish ambition.

CHALLENGE

Challenge

WHO in your life has received good news lately? In the space here, write her name and how you could actively, tangibly celebrate her this week. Could you comment on her post, drop flowers on her doorstep, or take her to lunch? Try one of your ideas and see if it doesn't reduce envy's grip on your heart.

1. Write the name of a person who comes to mind.

Who in my life has received good news recently?

2. Check the way you plan to celebrate her or write your own idea below.

☐ SEND HER FLOWERS

☐ WRITE HER A SNAIL-MAIL NOTE

☐ COMMENT ON HER SOCIAL MEDIA POST

☐ TAKE HER FOR COFFEE

☐

DAY THREE

And let us consider how we may spur one another on toward love and good deeds, not giving up meeting together, as some are in the habit of doing, but encouraging one another—and all the more as you see the Day approaching.
- Hebrews 10:24-25

HAVE you ever met a natural-born encourager? My friend Donna is like that. Here's the birthday message I got from her last May:

"Thought you should know that all day long I will have my headlights on, windows down, waving at all the bystanders, and blowing my car horn, having my own parade to celebrate the day your were born and the great gift God gave to the world when he designed you and placed you here on planet Earth!"

And that's just part of the message! Donna Dee knows how to love and encourage others well; I want to grow up to be just like her.

We've been working this week on celebrating others out loud, on purpose, and with action. Today's verse challenges us to do it proactively. Celebrating a friend *after* her success loosens envy's grip. But . . .

Encouraging your friend along her path to success can prevent envy altogether.

"Meeting together"—over coffee, at the playground, on the phone—to pray and encourage each other makes you a partner in your friend's success. And the door gets slammed in the face of jealousy, envy, and comparison. This is community and friendship at its best.

PRAYER:
Father, I'm so grateful for the people who have cheered me on to past achievements with their prayers, text messages, and affirming notes. Show me how to be the encourager my friends, family, and co-workers need to accomplish the big things you've planned for them.

CHALLENGE

Challenge

WHAT are you doing to proactively encourage and celebrate your friends? If this doesn't come naturally to you, start by writing out a plan to really invest in one friend. Who is she, and what could you do that would make her day? Maybe coordinate a weekly chat with her or send her regular notes of encouragement.

1. Write in the name of a person who comes to mind.

Who is the Holy Spirit nudging you to encourage?

2. What would it look like to be her unexpected cheer-leader? Use the blank page to brainstorm ways to celebrate her.

DAY FOUR

*The harvest is great, but the workers are few. So pray
to the Lord who is in charge of the harvest; ask him to
send more workers into his fields.*
- Luke 10:2

PART of what makes it so hard to celebrate someone else is that the enemy is whispering to us the lie that everything—success, opportunity, praise—is in limited supply.

I'm a foster mom and was recently invited to speak at a conference about orphan care. As I read the bios of the other speakers in the conference book, I found myself thinking, *Do I have anything to say compared to these other amazing speakers?* When I dig into that, I must have been hoping that my insights and stories would be better or more powerful or more motivating than theirs. Yuck! I was stuck in the lie that the other speakers' success would somehow leave less for me.

But our God's economy is one of abundance—"the harvest is great."

Seeing a friend win at something doesn't diminish your shot at success.

There is enough to go around; in fact, there is so much to go around that today's verse reminds us our prayer should really be for more friends to find success putting their gifts to use for God.

"All tides rise when we see a sister making this world a better place with her gifts."
—Lysa TerKeurst

PRAYER:
Jesus, how easy it is to slip into the lie that success is scarce. I want to cheer for my friends, so I pray today that you would bless with great success those around me who are putting their gifts to use for you.

CHALLENGE

Challenge

GOD GIFTS us uniquely. Write down a few ways God has gifted you and give thanks for how he made you. Then spend a few minutes celebrating the unique gifts of a friend or two.

1. As hard as it is, think about three things you're good at and write them below.

Three things I'm good at are:
Examples: cooking, planning, organizing

2. Think about two of your friends. Fill in the blanks below with what they're REALLY great at. And maybe shoot each one a text telling her just how great you think she is. You'll make her day!

My friend is really great at

My friend is really great at

DAY FIVE

Jesus replied: "Love the Lord your God with all your heart and with all your soul and with all your mind." This is the first and greatest commandment. And the second is like it: "Love your neighbor as yourself." All the Law and the Prophets hang on these two commandments.
- Matthew 22:37-40

WE'VE talked a lot about your incredible value and worth in God's eyes; he has called you "his masterpiece." But here's the catch about that truth: it applies to everyone. God loves your best friend, your fellow carpool moms, and your colleagues as much as he loves you. So when we choose to honor and celebrate one another, we are honoring and celebrating someone precious to God.

If you're a mom, don't you just love it when other people applaud your children? Could it be that God, our Father, feels that way about us? Can't you just picture him beaming like a proud parent when he hears us applaud one another?

In today's verse, Jesus gives us two action steps—love God and love your neighbor. But let's zoom in on the five little words wedged in the middle: "the second is like it." In other words, the second command is equal or on par with the first. Meaning that it is just as important to love one another as it is to love God.

Let's love others well by applauding their accomplishments and celebrating their skills.

Doing so serves us well by cleaning out envy and jealousy, but Jesus reminds us that it also serves God well.

> **PRAYER:**
> Father, what a powerful thought that we are each so precious and valuable to you. Show me how I can celebrate and applaud others in my life—out of love and honor for them and for you.

CHALLENGE

Challenge

WHAT is one thing you can do today to "love your neighbor as yourself"? Write it in this space and then do it. You'll be glad you did.

1. Answer the questions below.

Who do I know that could use some love today?

What is something I could do for her today?

2. So, will you do it? What are you waiting for? Come back later when you've done it, and think through these questions.

How did you feel before you served her?
Example: anxious, nervous

How did you feel while you were serving her?
Example: awkward, helpful

How did you feel after you served her?
Example: useful, fulfilled

How do you think she feels now?
Example: grateful, humble

DAY SIX

But he said to me, "My grace is sufficient for you, for my power is made perfect in weakness. Therefore I will boast all the more gladly about my weaknesses, so that Christ's power may rest on me."
- 2 Corinthians 12:9

IF WE IMAGINE each of our skills, gifts, past experiences, and passions filling the nooks of a bookshelf, there are some pieces that we'd prefer to tuck away in the overlooked corners of the shelf, aren't there? Maybe your story includes abuse. Maybe your marriage ended or your child was born with special needs. Maybe entire seasons of your life have been swallowed by addiction.

Comparison may be whispering to you the lie that those pieces of your story should be kept hidden— that admitting them out loud would be intentionally pointing out that you don't measure up, that you aren't perfect enough.

Can I suggest that God may want to move those pieces of your story right to the front of your bookshelf?

God can leverage and use the unpolished, imperfect parts of your story.

They can illustrate for others his power to comfort, sustain, heal, and redeem.

Admitting the less-than-perfect parts of you is hard in a culture of comparison. But God promises, "My grace is sufficient for you." So go ahead and share your story—all of your story.

PRAYER:
Heavenly Father, it seems a little crazy to me that you're interested in taking the broken stuff of my life and using it for good. But since you say so, I'm offering all of it to you now. Please give me new eyes to see my story the way you do and to see how I can put it to good use.

CHALLENGE

Challenge

DO YOU have a friend who has been transparent with a tough piece of her past? Use the space below to process what you can learn from her example.

Take some time to think and journal through these questions.

> Who is a person I know that has been
> transparent with a tough part of her past?

> What parts of my life do I hide
> from others?

Why don't I want anyone to know?

What could I do to let God use and leverage my experiences?

DAY SEVEN

Because of the Lord's great love we are not consumed,
for his compassions never fail. They are new every
morning; great is your faithfulness. I say to myself,
"The Lord is my portion; therefore I will wait for him."
- Lamentations 3:22-24

I HAVE some good news and some bad news.

Let's get the bad news out of the way first. Conquering comparison is a race with no finish line. We can create new habits and avoid specific triggers, but the truth is, comparison will perpetually be a tension to manage.

Maybe you started the school year or the diet committed to avoiding the comparison trap. Then one conversation or one glance at her outfit (that didn't include threadbare yoga pants like yours) and you were right back in the grip of insecurity and envy.

Want the good news? God gives us unlimited tries

to get it right. We don't have to be consumed and debilitated by our failures.

God is compassionate. It breaks his heart to see us struggle.

When comparison makes us feel lousy about ourselves, the last thing God wants is for us to then feel bad that we can't break this bad habit once and for all.

There may not be a finish line in sight, but the daily race to leverage—rather than compare—what you have is a worthy one.

PRAYER:
God, thank you for offering fresh starts. Thank you for loving me despite—and in the midst of—this struggle. I would be so defeated without your compassion and faithfulness.

CHALLENGE

Challenge

WHEN jealousy, envy, and comparison pop up, use the last part of today's passage as your in-the-moment prayer: "The Lord is my portion; therefore I will wait for him." Write or maybe even draw what this verse means to you.

"the lord is my portion, therefore I wait for him."

LAMENTATIONS 3:24

Use this space to write or draw this verse. Feel free to write it out word for word, or draw whatever comes to your mind.

CLOSING THOUGHTS

closing thoughts

by Sandra Stanley

Well, you made it!

I think it's safe to assume you now realize that comparison truly is a trap. It is absolutely a thief of your joy and peace. I bet you've also discovered that you're not alone! We all struggle because we live in a culture of comparison that seems committed to destroying our joy and peace with simple glances at our computer screens or smartphones. This age of awareness takes comparison to a new level and propels us toward jealousy, insecurity, and even financial irresponsibility.

Thankfully, we don't have to live this way. We don't have to be jealous of someone who has more. We don't have to hope a friend fails so we can feel better about ourselves. We don't have to make irresponsible purchases in order to be envied. We don't have to push our boyfriends, husbands, or kids to be more and do more so we can feel satisfied that everyone is properly impressed.

Since wrapping up the writing and recording of this study, I can't even count the number of times comparison has come creeping back into my mind and heart. Its constant attempts

to derail my peace, my contentment, and my joy are reminders of its insidious persistence. But now I have some tools!

While there is certainly no finish line when it comes to conquering comparison, I hope these last 28 days have given you some tools too. The habit of spending daily time in Scripture is one I pray you will continue. There is certainly no better way to combat comparison. Keep this devotional/journal somewhere close so you will be reminded, even by the title on the cover, that comparison is a trap.

Most importantly, I hope you walk away from these weeks with a renewed assurance that your worth is off the charts because you belong to a heavenly Father who says, "You are fine because you are mine."

I'm so glad you took the time to do this study. Always remember—there is no win in comparison!

Sandra

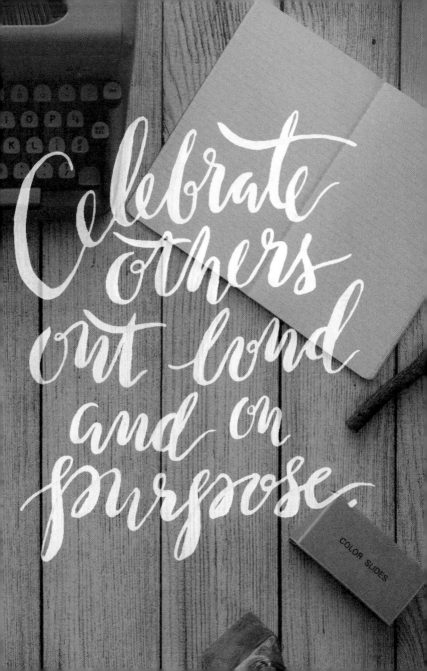

Cut along the line and frame the backside of this page.

Leader's Guide

LEADING THE SESSIONS

SESSION ONE:

Session 1 brings out the tension we feel as we compare ourselves to others. This tension is not intended to be resolved; it sets up the discussion for Session 2. Allow your group to explore and remain in this tension. Also, be aware that question two has the potential to bring to light some significant childhood wounds. If this happens, affirm what is shared and continue to create a safe environment for people to share.

SESSION TWO:

While Session 2 walks us through the idea that we should look up (to God) rather than around, it's not easy to reprogram. Allow your group to explore the obstacles (earthly parents, early influences, etc.). Reiterate that anything that contradicts the Scripture verses is a lie. These verses are the true and accurate view. The devotions will set up how to replace the opposing beliefs with truth.

SESSION THREE:

Session 3 sets up the false idea that "God owes me." It might be hard for some to admit, but it's okay to be mad at God. They are in good company. Moses got mad at God (Exodus 5:22–23); Jeremiah got mad at God (Jeremiah 20:7–18). They don't need to move through this quickly. God can handle their anger. The truth is that even in the hardest circumstances, God is near (Psalm 34:18), and he is our Comforter (2 Corinthians 1:3–5).

SESSION FOUR:

The antidote for comparison is twofold: celebration of others and leveraging what God has given each of us. Make sure to spend time on both ideas. This is also a great time to go back through the different Challenge sections and see the progress that has been made. A perfect time to celebrate!

GENERAL GROUP TIPS

If you find yourself as the lead facilitator of the Discussion Questions, here are three things to consider:

CULTIVATE DISCUSSION.
It is the ideas of everyone in the group that make a group meeting successful. Your role as the leader is to create an environment in which people feel safe to share their thoughts.

STAY ON TRACK.
While you want to leave space for group members to think through the discussion, make sure the conversation is contributing to the topic being discussed that session. Don't let it veer off on tangents. Go with the flow, but be ready to nudge the conversation in the right direction when necessary.

PRAY.
This is the most important thing you can do as a leader and as a group. Pray that God is not only present at your group meetings, but that he is directing them.